Straight
from
The Heart

Poems
by
KERRY LEWIS

LEATHERS
PUBLISHING

A division of Squire Publishers, Inc.
4500 College Blvd.
Leawood, KS 66211
1/888/888-7696

Copyright 2000
Printed in the United States

ISBN: 1-58597-062-X

LEATHERS
PUBLISHING

A division of Squire Publishers, Inc.
4500 College Blvd.
Leawood, KS 66211
1/888/888-7696

ACKNOWLEDGEMENTS

The author acknowledges with grateful appreciation the assistance of all those who helped make this book possible.

My wife, Lynn, always supportive and always persistent that I get something published.

The driving force of sons and daughters who always need something.

All the friends and relatives who have supported my endeavors and given me inspiration.

                                              Thanks,
                                              Kerry

VERSES

I've written about everything,
   holidays and winter scenes,
Summer storms and winter nights
   and all my secret dreams.

My verse on love alone
   could fill a lengthy book.
While sitting at a wooden desk,
   I've described a mountain brook.

With flowing pen I've etched
   the ocean and the sea,
of valleys and the mountains
   and eagles flying free.

With pen in hand
   I've watched my child at night
and written all my thoughts
   until the dawning light.

From childhood dreams
   to the death we fear,
of love and romance,
   heartbreak and tears.

Yesterdays and tomorrow,
   of time that never ends,
as well as the golden leaves of autumn
   and sharing time with friends.

With a heavy heart
    I've written verse so true,
and of special moments in my life,
    I've written of them, too.

Straight from the heart
    I've laid it all bare,
recorded forever
    for you to share.

TABLE OF CONTENTS

LOVE
- Yesterday's Love 2
- Will You? 3
- You Don't Really Know 4
- Yesterday's Dreams 5
- I Love 6
- How Much …? 7
- Love Me 8

NATURE
- The Sea 10
- Full Moon Rising 11
- Autumn 12
- Winter 13
- Low Country Fog 14
- Dawn 15
- Winter Life 16
- Dog Days of Summer 17
- The Forest 18
- Country Evening 19
- Ozark Country 20
- Nature 21
- Spring 22

CHILDREN
- To a Twelve-Year-Old 24
- My Little Child 25
- A Box of Souvenirs 26
- Daddy 28
- Sadness 29
- Through My Eyes 30

LIFE

Yesterday 32
As I walk Alone 33
The Rat Race 34
Today 35
Fiction 36
The Gray Ghost.................................... 37
The Wise Old Man 38
Alone 39
Shadows of Progress 40
Decisions 41
The Old Picture Album 42
Reflections 44
Old Friend 45
Home 46
My Scrapbook 47
Modern Day Life 48

DEATH — IMMORTALITY

Before I die 50
Life's Journey 51
Taps 52
The Yard 53
The Hero 54
The Old Church 55
An Old Wooden Church 56

Love

*If fun is good, then truth is better,
and love, the best of all.*
— *Thackery*

YESTERDAY'S LOVE

Yesterday's love just passed me by,
awakening memories from the past,
Like a faded rose
in a crystal sherry glass.

Two lovers long ago,
now strangers on the street;
What memories crossed her mind
as we unexpected meet?

For one moment, eye to eye,
did she even recognize
the one who held her close
and listened to her lies?

Were her eyes wet with tears
of memories from the past,
Or was it from the pain
of a love that didn't last?

Answers I will never know
for she didn't even speak,
Just a shadow of a smile
while passing on a busy street.

WILL YOU?

Will you still love me
   when we've grown old?
Will your love stay warm
   and never grow cold?

Will you keep your promise
   to carry my name
And share all the burdens
   if I do the same?

Will you love me as much
   when I make you mad
And understand me
   when I'm feeling bad?

Will you love me tomorrow
   as much as today
And promise me always
   you'll not run away?

If you can say "yes"
   and the answer be true,
Then you should know
   that's why "I love you."

YOU DON'T REALLY KNOW

You don't really know . . .
   and you can't fully understand
      How much I love you.

You are first a woman . . .
   and then my wife
      Always a part of my life.

You're complicated . . .
   unpredictable and vulnerable.
      I'm just an ordinary man.

With eyes red from tears . . .
   You say you're sorry
      for something you haven't done.

Your love fills me with desire . . .
   Only you can share
      my private dreams.

You'll never know
   nor fully understand
      How much I love you.

YESTERDAY'S DREAMS

Nobody knows
   what tomorrow brings . . .
Romance and Love
   or broken dreams.

A warm smile
   from a stranger's face,
Or a poor man wandering
   from place to place.

Someone in need
   of your offered hand,
A token of Love
   that they'll understand.

A sunshine day
   or cloudy sky;
Don't let today
   just pass you by.

Don't live today
   on yesterday's dreams;
For nobody knows
   what tomorrow brings.

I LOVE . . .

I love . . .
    A rainbow in the sky,
    An eagle flying high,
    Violets of darkest blue,
        and **you**.

I love . . .
    A baby's blue-eyed stare,
    The blinding ocean glare,
    A field of waving wheat,
        and moments when we meet.

I love . . .
    A yellow moon at night,
    Dogs that never bite,
    The sound of a country fair,
        and happy hours we share.

I love . . .
    A child's simple embrace
    With teardrops on his face.
    A love that's always true,
        and always there is **you**.

HOW MUCH . . . ?

How much do I love you . . . ?
   I don't really know,
You're always with me
   wherever I go.

I love you more today
   but less than tomorrow,
As much in happiness
   as I would in sorrow.

I love you in pre-dawn hours
   as much as tonight,
Your whisper-soft touch
   while holding me tight.

I love you as much
   whenever you're crying
Just as I would laughing,
   in sickness or dying.

How much do I love you . . . ?
   I can't really say,
But I know it's more
   than I did yesterday.

LOVE ME

My love is like a flower . . .
   I need your attention each day.
Just touch me and tell me
   in your special way.

Make me feel happy
   when I'm really depressed.
When I'm worn and tired,
   give me comfort and rest.

If I'm over burdened . . .
   carry more than your share.
Should I become hurt,
   show that you really care.

It's not very much
   to say "I love you,"
But it takes more effort
   to show that we do.

Nature

*Poems are made by fools like me,
but only God can make a tree.*
—Joyce Kilmer

THE SEA

The Sea, as old as time,
    never stays the same;
With changing shape and color
    it plays an endless game.

Like fingers, reaching, grasping,
    the waves attack the shore,
Then retreat in haste
    to form the charge once more.

With a sound like distant cannon
    they explode on broken reefs,
Disintegrate to foam, dissolve,
    the endless cycle, once more, complete.

FULL MOON RISING

With a full moon rising
   to light up the sky,
the dark shadows
   have no place to hide.

The night creatures come forth
   to howl at the moon
and play hide and seek
   on a bright night in June.

Then a black cloud forms
   and brings forth lightning;
Mother Nature's jealous
   of a full moon rising.

AUTUMN

The green leaves of summer
    now turning red and gold
Foreshadow the coming winter
    of snow and bitter cold.

The grey squirrels leap
    among the autumn leaves
In search of hard nuts
    to cache for the coming freeze.

The cows and sheep
    are growing shaggy coats,
While the farmer works late
    to harvest winter oats.

The geese are in flight,
    all southward bound,
While the night gives cover
    to their passing sound.

The work day grows shorter
    with darkness by dinner;
And the green leaves of summer
    fall silently, for winter.

WINTER

I view the winter morning
    through a frosty window pane,
As a field of frozen corn
    stiffly guards the rutted lane.

Icicles formed last night
    now hang from barren trees;
Like winter guests
    they take the place of leaves.

A gust of icy wind
    blows across the lake,
To freeze the hinges
    on a weather-beaten gate.

Snowdrifts, white as cotton,
    blanket the rocky land;
A picture perfect morning
    in a winter wonderland.

LOW COUNTRY FOG

In early morning hours
   it rises from the ground,
Like a haunting ghost,
   drifting without a sound.

Slipping among the trees
   it covers the cypress logs.
Nature's protective blanket
   for low country bogs.

Eerie noises,
   should you listen close,
As the swamp creatures stir
   beneath her cloak.

The slap of water
   from a striking bass,
And the swish of reeds
   from a water rat.

The slithering sound
   of a passing snake,
Casting the slightest ripple
   within its wake.

Other creatures begin to stir,
   staking claim to a favorite log,
Protected from harm
   by the silent fog.

DAWN

Early morning hours of silence
   broken by wild geese flying,
As the night wind
   retires with a final sighing.

Daylight replaces the darkness
   as the night is done;
And the moon recedes
   to the rising sun.

A mockingbird calls,
   like a sentry on duty,
Awakening the world
   to witness the beauty.

WINTER LIFE

Long dark nights
   with a cold wind blowing;
Extra clothes . . .
   and heavy snowing.

Icy breath
   and frozen streams;
Feather beds
   for sleepy dreams.

Old pickup trucks
   with snow tread tires,
and drinking coffee
   by the cracklin' fires.

Idle chatter
   and whittling things
while making plans
   for the coming spring.

DOG DAYS OF SUMMER

Sultry, hot and humid.
    Dog days . . . Indian summer.
Storm clouds roll overhead
    and a distant sound of thunder.

Window units churning hard
    to produce a cooling breeze,
While the dogs lull panting
    in shade of drooping trees.

Boats shimmer in a heat wave
    reflected from the sun,
While on the beach, vacationers
    risk heat stroke in pursuit of fun.

Dusk brings relief from heat
    as the sun slips from the sky
While night life, sex and love
    ebb with the passing tide.

Sweat comes with the dawn
    as tempers explode like thunder,
Another routine day
    in a long hot summer.

THE FOREST

In the depth of the forest,
    below a giant redwood tree,
I breathed the scents of nature
    which lay about me.

The climbing thistle rose,
    the fern and ivy climb;
Hollyhock, oleander and greenbriar
    twist among the strawberry vine.

High overhead among the limbs
    the squirrels are hid from view,
As less timid birds fly by
    in a flash of red and blue.

The thump of a falling cone,
    a rustle in the leaves;
The living sounds of nature
    among the giant trees.

COUNTRY EVENING

Daylight hours grow short
   as summer turns to fall;
Among the fading leaves
   a "whippoorwill" calls.

In a river bottom field
   the corn stands shoulder-high,
As a cloud of black crows gather
   in the evening sky.

The river, swift and muddy,
   beneath the bridge so old,
Will become a winter playground
   when covered by the snow.

On a rocky ridge field,
   protected by the trees,
A crop of winter wheat
   shimmers in the breeze.

The early evening stars
   twinkle in the fading light,
As a golden "harvest moon"
   welcomes in the night.

OZARK COUNTRY

Winding roads passing
   among the rocky hills;
sun bleached barns
   and homemade stills.

Countless country streams
   and spring-fed brooks;
plain old country folks
   with an honest, open look.

One-street towns
   with even stranger names,
and barefoot children
   content with made-up games.

General stores at crossroads
   with treasures from the past;
from trace-chains and collars
   to a feathered cowboy hat.

Sway back, empty churches
   among the towering trees,
while the long forgotten graveyard
   collects the falling leaves.

A grist mill still turning,
   powered by the quiet stream,
and the sorghum-press operated
   by a slow walking team.

Wild flowers grow
   among the giant oak tree,
and life changes slow
   in the Ozark country.

NATURE

Set your eyes upon a goal
    and reach toward a star.
We pass this way but once
    In search of riches near and far.

Our eyes are closed to wonders
    which we never take time to see,
Storm clouds drifting in blue skies
    and birds that fly so free.

Majestic peaks above green valleys
    all about us lie;
Yet we miss the simple beauty
    if we don't open up our eyes.

Make time to smell the flowers
    or fish a mountain stream,
And gaze upon the beauty
    of pine woods that are green.

We pass through life but once
    and we need a lot of cheer;
Take time to look at nature
    and feel the beauty which is near.

SPRING

Wildflowers slowly push
   through the warming earth,
While overhead, clouds scurry
   in an erratic course.

Young robins chirp
   in loud profusion
As a flock of jays
   add to wild confusion.

The sun climbs to the zenith
   and gently warms the earth.
After a long cold winter,
   Spring is bursting forth.

Children

Listen to a child and he will teach you something of love, faith and wonder.

— *Unknown*

TO A TWELVE-YEAR-OLD

How fast time passes
   and little girls grow.
From just a little baby
   to a twelve-year-old.

Your baby fingers
   once reached for mine,
And your sloppy kiss
   I loved just fine.

I bought your first dress,
   a silver spoon and cup.
You were just a baby
   I didn't want to grow up.

I spanked you some
   and dried your tears,
And loved you always
   through your childhood years.

You're a big girl now
   and I'm a little sad;
With your busy life
   there's little time for Dad.

MY LITTLE CHILD

Where have you gone,
   my little child,
With wind blown hair
   and sunny smile?

Where's the innocence
   and childish charm,
Your tears and kisses
   and the love so warm?

No more games
   or secrets shared;
No special words
   to show you've cared.

She's growing up . . .
   my little child;
And childish love
   is out of style.

A BOX OF SOUVENIRS

While searching in my attic
   I found a box from yesteryear,
filled to overflowing
   with countless souvenirs.

With a moment of hesitation
   to calm my trembling hand,
I thought of you,
   as only a father can.

This box from yesteryear
   filled with love, now growing old;
each piece, a part of you,
   a memory, from long ago.

A worn stuffed puppy dog
   with a silly, crooked smile;
Your special friend
   you played with for awhile.

This red-haired little doll
   with a faded, dirty dress,
You said you'd love forever
   and even named her "Bess."

I see a special card
   with a little written verse,
and this thing here
   was once your favorite purse.

I touch a string
   of imitation pearls,
and see so clear,
   a bunch of shiny curls.

A broken watch, a rusty ring,
   a pretty toy, I see;
I feel a deep sadness
   as a single tear falls free.

This music box,
   once shared your dreams;
I've wound it often,
   a thousand times, it seems.

I see a scarf,
   the color of spun gold,
and recall a winter day
   of snow and sleds and cold.

A picture from an album,
   a clover, pressed for luck,
and last, a golden heart,
   the key, forever stuck.

With a sigh, I close
   my box from yesteryear,
filled to overflowing
   with priceless souvenirs.

DADDY

How far the distant mountains
   which reach for the sky?
The sky itself . . .
   How high?

The ocean so beautiful,
   do you know how deep?
And all the fish . . .
   do they ever sleep?

Daddy, where do the stars go
   at break of day,
And the sun
   when it goes away?

Does the rain come from heaven,
   are clouds made of fluff?
Daddy, to answer my questions
   are you smart enough?

SADNESS

The silence is like a shadow
   weighing heavy on my mind.
Missing her is a sadness
   which hurts a hundred times.

Pieces of her life
   all about me lie,
And my eyes are clouded
   with tears I couldn't cry.

There's a scuffy pair of shoes
   and a sad old teddy bear;
A poster on the wall
   in a room she used to share.

Here's a ribbon and a bow,
   a pair of dirty jeans,
And on a crooked shelf
   her book of favorite dreams.

I look about the room
   at pictures on the wall,
And miss her merry laughter
   and wonder if she'll call.

How many years
   must I feel sad,
With one less daughter
   to call me "Dad"?

THROUGH MY EYES

Through my eyes, I see a child,
   growing more each day,
from an infant to a man,
   in a thousand different ways.

Through my eyes, I've watched you change
   from year to year;
and feel a little sadness
   that adulthood is growing near.

Through my eyes, I've shed a tear
   whenever you have cried,
and prayed you would succeed
   in all that you have tried.

Through my eyes, I've seen
   your disappointments and pain,
and shared your loss
   while playing life's cruel game.

Through my eyes I've seen
   the happiness we've shared,
and treasure little gifts
   that show you really cared.

Through these same eyes
   I'll see you grown, in time;
an honest, upright man,
   so proud that you are mine.

Most important, I know the joy
   you've brought into our lives,
your sunny smile, your growing love;
   Yes, son, I've seen it all; through my eyes.

Life

The man who tries to be good, loving and kind finds life, righteousness and honor.
— *Proverbs 21:21*

YESTERDAY

Yesterday, when I was young,
    all my dreams were gay.
I longed for peace of mind,
    the same as I do today.

Yesterday was full of joy
    with a full amount of cheer,
Unlike today, so afraid,
    growing old with fear.

Yesterday was sunshine,
    a sky of cloudless blue.
I'm older now,
    with doubts of what to do.

Yesterday, when I was young,
    adulthood was far away.
I've reached it now, and regret
    the games I didn't play.

AS I WALK ALONE

Sometimes I walk alone
   on a beach of shifting sand,
Immune to everyone
   as only dreamers can.

Often lost in a memory
   from a long forgotten past,
Or chasing an elusive dream
   which I know will never last.

My escape from all the problems,
   the worry and the strife;
From a load of responsibilities;
   the essence of my life.

A chance to count my blessings,
   to scheme and dream and plan,
As I walk alone
   on a beach of shifting sand.

THE RAT RACE

The buzzing of the clock
   starts a ringing in my head,
With an effort, I open eyes
   and stumble from my bed.

I feel my way
   across the cluttered floor
And crack my shins
   on the half open door.

With shaking hands
   I wash my face,
While the ticking clock
   sets the harried pace.

As I drink my coffee
   now thick and cold,
I wonder just what
   this day shall hold.

Daylight brings another day,
   and new decisions for me to face.
With a sigh, I say "good-bye"
   and say hello to the great "rat race."

TODAY

Today started like all others
   with buzzing alarms;
Foggy thoughts and dreams
   and sleepy yawns.

Dreading the day to come,
   I stumble from my bed.
Sleep begs for my return
   but I wash my face instead.

I tread slowly to the kitchen
   with just another yawn,
Fix my cup of coffee
   and face the coming dawn.

A quiet time of morning;
   ghostly, damp and grey.
Then I watched two squirrels
   at early morning play.

More awake, I realized
   the roses were in bloom;
And the grass much greener
   than it ever was at noon.

I felt my spirits lift
   in a different, peaceful way,
While watching the sun come up
   giving birth to another day.

FICTION

Books are full of dreams,
   of love and riches
      with no reference to pain.

The stories we read
   from the library hall . . .
      Love, adventure and fame!

Those stories are just fiction . . .
   A recluse from reality.
      The real life is not the same.

A better book is experience.
   Day by day, moment by moment,
      a gigantic, continuous chess game!

What consequence will you pay
   if you make a fatal move?
      You lose more than you gain!

Each day, a calculated risk . . .
   Unlike the library book . . .
      Fiction and Life are not the same.

THE GRAY GHOST

Once more it heads for sea,
   like a ghost upon the moors;
A battleship of gray
   bound for some distant shore.

The crowd upon the pier,
   saddened by their loss
Of fathers, sons and lovers,
   wave farewell in silent remorse.

With a shrill, short whistle
   the journey has begun;
And the gray ghost recedes
   into the setting sun.

THE WISE OLD MAN

We sat in the shade
   of a withered old tree;
The wise old man,
   his dog and me.

I'd listen to stories
   from a distant past,
Of quick earned fortunes
   which didn't last.

The mountains high
   that he had climbed,
And the gold and silver
   which he had mined.

He told me tales
   of foreign lands,
Where fortunes were buried
   in the hot desert sand.

He knew how to live
   in a land of snow,
And he guided my life
   and watched me grow.

He fed my dreams
   that set me free;
The wise old man,
   his dog and me.

ALONE

You're gone again . . .
   By now you're nearly home,
And I'm just sitting here
   once again, alone.

Alone I think best
   and often speak out loud,
Asking myself such questions
   like where, and when and how?

Where do I find happiness,
   will I always feel the same?
Why must I be the loser
   in another person's game?

How far must I travel
   and where must I go . . .
Would I be satisfied
   to find my El Dorado?

These questions, like others,
   urge me to roam,
When I'm just sitting here
   once again, alone.

SHADOWS OF PROGRESS

I can remember
   when the sun would shine,
And the wind would blow
   through a tall green pine.

You could catch a trout
   from a mountain stream
And walk in a field
   that was always clean.

High in the sky
   an eagle would be;
Like the wind and rain
   he was always free.

Now the sky is shadowed
   by a smoggy cloud,
Fed by the fires
   from a rowdy crowd.

The wild beasts are captured
   to live in a zoo;
An endangered species,
   they're protected from you.

The forests are ravished
   for the lumber so fine;
A world of beauty
   destroyed in a life time!

DECISIONS

Like a jigsaw puzzle
   I re-arrange my life
      and find some pieces missing.

Regardless of my strategy,
   some pieces never interlock
      and I'm left wishing.

But wishing sparks motivation
   which in turn leads to action . . .
      something I'm resisting.

For action can be costly,
   exciting, demanding, heartbreaking.
      Is it a chance worth taking?

THE OLD PICTURE ALBUM

While searching through an attic
   of old discarded junk,
I found a lot of memories
   locked in a dusty wooden trunk.

In an old picture album
   now faded with age,
I saw again, old pictures
   of us on every page.

How young we were,
   when life was just a game,
while hand in hand we walked
   never dreaming it would change.

As I turned the pages,
   old memories came flashing past
of two young lovers
   with a love that wouldn't last.

From a high school graduation
   to a war ship upon the sea,
a lifetime of memories
   on file for all to see.

Our first Christmas together
   we smiled and laughed a lot,
an Easter Sunday morning
   at our favorite picnic spot.

Pictures of our old Chevy
   and playing football in the park,
laughing at a picture show
   and kissing in the dark.

A group of friends together
   to celebrate and play,
and I wonder what has happened
   and where they are today?

As the pictures continued
   to record the passing years,
I felt an old familiar feeling
   and my eyes were filled with tears.

When I turned the final page
   of the book of memories past
I smile with sad reflection
   of love that didn't last.

REFLECTIONS

My mind is like a mirror
   where I see reflections of the past . . .
the adolescent years
   with dreams that didn't last.

But I recall some good times
   I shared with childhood friends
when we lived in a dream world
   which we'll never see again.

Then came the growing years
   as I rushed to be a man,
not content to sit and wait,
   I hurried as only children can.

Expecting life to be like stories
   I'd read so many of . . .
filled with daring adventure,
   and always there was love.

Too soon those years were over
   and too quickly growing old,
how true the parable,
   all that glitters is not gold.

Now years later
   as I recall the past
of all the dreams and heartaches,
   only the memories really last.

OLD FRIEND

Here's to you, Old Friend,
   bottoms up one more time.
We've shared it all . . .
   right down the line.

We've talked all night,
   or so it seems,
From politics and love
   to our secret dreams.

We never argue,
   have no need to shout;
And you always agree
   whatever the subject's about.

You're really smart
   and up to date;
No frets or worries
   if you stay up late.

You understand me
   for you've made mistakes;
Whatever I do . . .
   you think it's great!

I can depend on you
   for you're always near.
Here's to you, my friend,
   in the long, tall mirror.

HOME

The old town looked the same
    as I stepped down from the train.
No one came running up to meet me,
    only strangers could I see.

I stood still and looked around
    at the buildings old and gray,
And memories came rushing back
    from a past so far away.

New buildings here, the old ones gone;
    I've been away so very long.
Fighting wars and growing old
    aren't like the stories you are told.

On my right, there's the park
    where lovers stroll just after dark.
On my left I see the stream
    where many hours I could dream.

Here's a street lined with trees,
    standing like sentries in the breeze.
With passing years, all things change,
    and I think of the girl that has my name.

I see the house all painted white,
    and through tears that blur my sight,
I see a girl and little boy;
    I call their name and cry with joy.

Then she is there at my side,
    my true love, with arms open wide.
No more will I roam . . .
    God, it's great to be home!

MY SCRAPBOOK

Looking through a scrapbook
 of pictures faded gray . . .
Brings back memories
 of long forgotten days.

Of a rundown farm
 I called my home,
Where my childhood games
 were played alone.

The hot summer days
 at a swimming hole,
And fishing by moonlight
 with my homemade pole.

The sweat and blisters
 from working in hay,
And the weary bones
 at the end of day.

The freezing wind
 with a bitter chill,
And long winter nights
 so crisp and still.

All these memories
 just stored away
In a ragged book . . .
 of pictures faded gray.

MODERN DAY LIFE

How calm I appear
   when I first wake up,
While inside I'm like a volcano
   about to erupt.

I face each day
   with such a perfect calm,
only to end the day
   with curse and frown.

With small infractions
   which tax my patience
I'm forced to abide
   my growing impatience.

When nightfall comes
   I've used my last reserve
and search with troubled dreams
   the rest which I deserve.

Death — Immortality

In one sense there is no death.

The life of a soul on earth lasts beyond his departure. You will always feel that life touching yours, that voice speaking to you, that spirit looking out of other eyes,t alking to you in the familiar things he touched, worked with, loved as familiar friends.

He lives on in your life and in the lives of all that knew him.

— Angelo Patri

BEFORE I DIE

High on a mountain
   stretching to the sky . . .
Let me see the world
   just once before I die.

Let me walk among the ferns
   in the shadow of the trees,
And feel the cooling touch
   of an early evening breeze.

Let me see the beauty
   of an early morning sunrise,
While the dew is on the roses
   so appealing to the eyes.

May I walk among the driftwood
   on a beach so high and dry,
Beside the rippling ocean
   over which the seagulls fly?

The raindrops on my face,
   are they teardrops that you cry?
There's so much more to do
   Just once . . . before I die.

LIFE'S JOURNEY

One step can start a journey,
    each step can be a mile;
Each mile filled with heartache
    and heartaches last awhile.

Awhile can seem a lifetime,
    a lifetime marked with tears;
Tears shed in loneliness
    as we journey through the years.

The years filled with doubts,
    the doubts of what to do,
As we blindly search for strength
    to see the journey through.

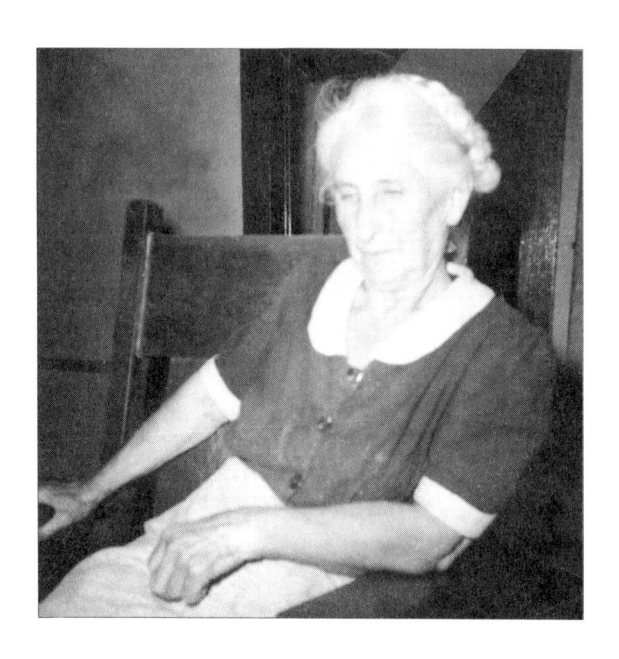

TAPS

As the setting sun
    sinks slowly in the west,
the soldier is gently lowered
    to a final, silent rest.

Old Glory, at last is folded,
    no longer to be a cloak,
draped across a coffin
    like a hero's overcoat.

The color guard is ready
    to fire the final shot,
as the widow hugs her child
    with tears she cannot stop.

The bugler blows his horn,
    a plaintive, lonely sound.
Welcome home, poor soldier,
    from a distant battleground.

THE YARD

How silent the yard
   where children never play;
And the green grass
   looks like carpet every day.

As I walk among the markers
   of marble, stone and clay,
I read the epitaphs
   from by-gone days.

I wonder about the ghosts
   of people laid to rest,
Each and every one
   dressed in Sunday best.

Some were rich
   and others rather poor;
The famous, now a name
   and really nothing more.

Everyone is finally equal
   when side by side they lay,
In a yard of grass
   where children never play.

THE HERO

His plane was met today
   with his family crying tears
and a crowd of special friends
   all wanting to be near.

The Captain spoke with pride
   about this soldier's life,
but I could hear more clearly,
   the crying of the young man's wife.

The officer told stories
   of a war in some foreign land,
but all I can remember
   was holding his small hand.

The battles that he fought
   and the men he led in war
earned him great respect
   and another Silver Star.

The ribbons on his chest
   were proof he was a man,
but to a grieving father
   they didn't mean a damn.

The flag was folded neatly
   and presented with great pride
and accepted proudly by his mother
   with tears she couldn't hide.

The rifles fired a volley
   and Taps was sounded slow;
another son was honored
   where Heroes always go.

THE OLD CHURCH

The old church stood alone
   among the trees and vines,
Built, used and abandoned,
   neglected by mankind.

The door stands partially open
   on a broken, rusty hinge,
an open invitation
   to the wildlife that enter in.

The seats are now decayed
   where families sat side by side,
and listened to the sermons
   or the mockingbird outside.

The floor of solid oak,
   once laid with loving care,
now lies warped and broken
   in need of much repair.

The window in the east,
   where the rising sun would show,
now stands paneless
   and lets in the rain and snow.

Once this old church
   was the strongest of its kind,
now a prime example
   when neglected for a time.

AN OLD WOODEN CHURCH

In an old churchyard
   I walked today,
among the stones
   so old and gray.

On 'stones worn smooth
   from nature's wind and rain
were the names from history . . .
   Gadsden, Moultrie, Payne.

The wooden church,
   once filled on Sunday,
stands long abandoned
   with signs of slow decay.

Imported stained glass windows
   from far across the sea
are now just remnants
   of what they used to be.

Inside, the handmade benches
   set upon a cold stone floor
in quiet anticipation
   of crowds that come no more.